Fondue

Fondue

Delicious recipes for easy entertaining

Lorraine Turner

p

This is a Parragon Publishing Book
First published in 2005

Parragon Publishing
Queen Street House
4 Queen Street
Bath
BA1 1HE, UK

Copyright © Parragon 2005

ISBN: 1-40545-832-1

Printed in China

Author: Lorraine Turner
Editor: Fiona Biggs
Designed by Fiona Roberts
Photography: Calvey Taylor-Haw
Home Economist: Ruth Pollock

Notes for the Reader
This book uses both imperial and US cup measurements. All spoon measurements are level; teaspoons are assumed to be 5 ml, and tablespoons are assumed to be 15 ml. Unless otherwise stated, milk is assumed to be full fat, individual vegetables such as potatoes are medium, and pepper is freshly ground black pepper. Recipes using raw or very lightly cooked eggs should be avoided by infants, the elderly, pregnant women, convalescents and anyone suffering from an illness. Pregnant and breastfeeding women are advised to avoid eating peanuts and peanut products. The times given are an approximate guide only. Preparation times differ according to the techniques used by different people and the cooking times may also vary from those given. Optional ingredients, variations, or serving suggestions have not been included in the calculations.

Contents

INTRODUCTION   PAGE 6

CHEESE FONDUES   PAGE 12

STOCK FONDUES   PAGE 38

SIZZLERS AND DIPPING SAUCES   PAGE 58

DESSERT FONDUES   PAGE 82

INDEX   PAGE 96

INTRODUCTION

It's great that fondues are back in fashion, as they are one of the easiest and most delightful ways of sharing a meal with family and friends.

They were hugely popular during the 1960s and 1970s, yet have been subject to all manner of insults since the novelty of cooking at the table wore off in the following decade. In fact, they have a longer and more venerable history than this would suggest.

Switzerland is credited with the invention of the cheese fondue. In essence, this consists of one or more cheeses melted with white wine and mixed with other flavorings. It is served in a pottery dish that can be placed over a spirit burner to keep it hot. Dippers—at their simplest just pieces of bread—are speared onto forks and used to scoop up the delicious mixture. In practice, the variety of cheese fondues is quite astonishing and, right from the start, both France and Italy enthusiastically adopted the idea, using their own local cheeses, wines, and flavorings.

Stock fondue is something of a misnomer as nothing is actually melted. Rather, pieces of meat, poultry, seafood, and vegetables are dipped into a pot of simmering broth. The morsels for spearing and cooking in the stock may be marinated first and are often served with a dipping sauce.

Oil fondues, inspired by their cheese ancestors, involve spearing pieces of meat, poultry, fish, seafood, or, more rarely, vegetables and cooking them in a metal pot of oil

kept hot over a spirit burner. They are then served with a choice of sauces and condiments. The Japanese refined this technique by coating the dippers in batter before cooking them to produce tempura.

Finally, the sweet fondues served for dessert are usually based on chocolate or syrup and dippers can range from pieces of fresh fruit to cookies and cubes of cake.

What's cooking?

The sheer simplicity of a fondue means that all the ingredients must be of the finest quality. This applies both to the ingredients for the cheese sauce or stock and the dippers. A flavorless cheese and acid wine will not improve with heating and there is no incentive to dip flaccid or dried-up vegetables into a pot of hot stock, let alone eat them.

A cheese with good melting qualities is a pre-requisite for a cheese fondue. Predictably, many Swiss cheeses, such as Emmental and Appenzeller, are ideal. Similar French and Italian cheese, from Comté to fontina, also work well. The French developed fondues made with creamy cheeses, such as Brie, used in combination with semihard ones, such as Beaufort. A wide variety of cheese has been used in the recipes in this book and you can experiment easily by substituting another cheese of the same type to insure the fondue has the right consistency.

As cheese fondues don't really cook the dippers, you cannot use completely raw ingredients for them. The classic dipper is bread, and other possibilities include cured ham, salami, cooked meat, lightly cooked or blanched vegetables, and some kinds of fruit, such as apples.

Both stock and oil fondues are kept at a higher temperature than cheese fondues and do involve cooking. It is necessary to make the stock—a cube or powder will not do—as this is the central part of the whole dish. In Asia, after the stock has been enriched as a result of the various dippers being cooked in it, it is served as soup at the end of the meal. Fortunately, making stock is quite easy, although you do need time for all the flavors to mingle during cooking. However, as many stocks for fondues are vegetable based, regardless of whether the dippers are meat, this is not so time-consuming as it might seem. Always use vegetables in peak condition for the best flavor. If a basic stock is required as an individual ingredient of the final broth, bouillon cubes and powder can be used.

The oil recommended for oil fondues in this book is peanut because it has a high smoke point—it doesn't burn or catch fire easily—and its mild flavor does not interfere with the taste of what it's cooking. Other suitable oils include sunflower, safflower, and corn oil. Olive oil has a much lower smoke point and a very distinctive flavor, so it is less suitable.

Raw dippers need to cook quite quickly. Meat should, therefore, be from prime cuts, such as chicken breast portions or sirloin steak. Firm, quick-cooking vegetables,

Types of fondue

Fondues are sold as sets containing a spirit burner, usually with a metal tray for it to stand on, a metal or ceramic pot to contain the cheese, stock, oil, or dessert sauce, and a stand or trivet to support the pot. Burners are usually fueled by methylated spirit, which should be handled with care, and the flame can be controlled by opening and closing vents. For some fondues, such as chocolate-based ones, the heat from a night-light is all that is required.

Cheese fondues are best served in a ceramic pot as they can burn onto the base of metal ones. Stock and oil fondues, on the other hand, require higher temperatures and should be served in a metal pot—stainless steel or enameled cast iron. Dessert fondues are variable—those based on chocolate are best in a ceramic pot, but toffee-like fondues work well in a metal one.

Using the fondue

Fondues are great fun and invariably stimulate table talk, but there are some sensible precautions to take to avoid spills, accidents, or burns. It is essential that the fondue is stable and will not tip over. It should be within easy reach of all diners. If you are planning to serve more than about six people, it is worth investing in a second fondue set. If there are lots of forks full of dippers in the pot, the temperature will be lowered, everything will take a long time to cook, and, as well as the boredom factor, there is a risk

such as mushrooms and broccoli, are perfect, and seafood is always a good choice. Vegetarians should not overlook tofu, which also works very well when used in both stock and oil fondues.

Dessert fondues also require the finest-quality ingredients. Chocolate will not melt properly unless it has a minimum of 50 percent cocoa solids. Semisweet chocolate is usually used for the best flavor and color. White chocolate is totally unsuitable. Cookies and cakes should be fresh, with a texture that contrasts deliciously with the fondue and fruit should be ripe and in peak condition. Like cheese fondues, dessert fondues don't really cook the dippers.

of undercooking, which can be a health hazard in the case of poultry, sausages, and pork.

If there's room on the table, it's worth dividing the dippers among a number of plates so that they are within easy reach of everyone. This avoids passing dishes backward and forward over the pot and also gives everyone the widest choice.

If you are using a spirit burner, fill it according to the manufacturer's instructions somewhere other than at the table. Place it in position before lighting it—once lit, do not leave it unattended. Never leave children alone with a hot fondue.

Prepare the fondue in an ordinary pan rather than in the fondue pot itself. This avoids splashes that could burn and create a most unappetizing smell and appearance. Using a larger pan than the fondue pot itself for preparation also insures that you have plenty of room for stirring, whisking, and so on. You can preheat the fondue pot before use if you want to. For stock fondues, fill the pot two-thirds full and for dessert and cheese fondues fill it no more than three-fourths full. For oil fondues, fill it no more than one-third full and then heat the oil on the stove until it reaches the required temperature. This is usually 375°F/190°C or until a cube of bread browns in 30 seconds. Unless the fondue pot has heatproof handles, use oven mitts to carry it.

The long, color-coded forks provided with the fondue set and available separately in batches of six are designed for cooking only. When removed from the fondue pot they will be very hot and could burn the mouth. They also have sharp prongs designed for impaling chunks of meat, so a stabbed tongue could be a most unpleasant result. Finally, returning a fork that has been in your mouth to a communal cooking pot is likely to put the other diners off their food. Provide ordinary table forks for all the diners and warn them about the heat and sharpness of the fondue forks. In particular, keep an eye on any children.

Preparing food

The idea of the fondue is that guests are presented with an appetizing array of dippers—often raw—that they can cook themselves and then eat immediately. Small pieces cook faster than larger ones and this is an important concern with such things as chicken that need to be cooked all the way through. Cut meat and poultry into neat, bite-size cubes. Leave small vegetables, such as mushrooms and cherry tomatoes, whole. Cut larger vegetables into bite-size pieces and separate broccoli and cauliflower into flowerets. If you are serving a selection of dippers—and that's part of the fun—try to make them all about the same size so that guests can thread two or three different morsels onto their forks and cook them simultaneously.

Meat should be boneless and trimmed of all visible fat. Chicken looks more attractive if the skin has been removed. It is a matter of choice whether you present cooked or raw shrimp. Cooked shrimp require hardly any time in the fondue pot but this does mean they can quickly become overcooked and lose their flavor and texture. Fish is less suitable for fondues than other ingredients. If you are going to serve it, use firm, fresh fillets, skinned and cut into bite-size pieces. Inspect it very carefully for pin bones. However, fish balls and mini fish patties make lovely dippers.

Store prepared vegetables individually in plastic bags in the salad drawer of the refrigerator. Remove food from the refrigerator about 30 minutes before you intend to serve. Chilled food will take a lot longer to cook than food that is at room temperature. If meat or seafood has been marinating, drain it well before placing it on the serving dish and, in the case of oil fondues, pat it dry with paper towels to avoid spitting oil during cooking.

Do spare a thought for suitable accompaniments. Crusty bread, mixed greens, rice and pasta salads, and baked potatoes are all very easy to prepare. French fries are popular with oil fondues.

Hints and tips

Before using your fondue set for the first time, read the manufacturer's instructions.

Tablecloths are best avoided as an inadvertent tug can destabilize the fondue.

Cut ingredients for dippers into bite-size pieces but no smaller. Otherwise, they will disintegrate.

Always use fresh oil every time you have an oil fondue. Recycled cooking oil, however well you try to filter it, will probably be tainted and is more likely to burn.

◎ Never overfill the spirit burner or the fondue pot.

If the burner springs a leak, smother the flames with a pan lid, upturned skillet, or a similar large, metal container. Do not throw water on the flames.

Keep an eye on the temperature of the fondue pot and adjust the heat by using the vents on the burner.

Use potato nest fryers for small dippers, such as nuts, that cannot easily be speared on a fork. This device consists of a hinged inner and outer basket which, when partly filled, can be held in place by a ring which fits over both handles. It has a very long handle to protect hands from the heat.

◎ If any dippers are lost in the pot, scoop them out with a slotted spoon, especially from oil fondues, to prevent them from burning and tainting the rest of the fondue.

◎ When the meal is finished, extinguish the burner immediately using the snuffer provided.

Care of the fondue

Allow the fondue pot to cool completely after an oil fondue, then dispose of the oil safely. Do not pour it down the sink. The pots may be left to soak in hot water or washed immediately. Enamel-coated cast-iron fondue pots are not usually dishwasher safe.

CHAPTER 1: CHEESE FONDUES

GRUYÈRE WITH ASPARAGUS

This classic fondue features four different cheeses and has a wonderfully rich flavor which is perfectly matched with luxurious asparagus dippers.

|◎| Serves 4

Preparation time: 10–15 minutes

Cooking time: 15–20 minutes

Ingredients

1 garlic clove, peeled and halved

generous 1¾ cups dry white wine

5 tbsp brandy

14 oz/400 g Gruyère cheese, grated

7 oz/200 g Emmental cheese, grated

3½ oz/100 g Parmesan cheese, grated

2 tbsp cornstarch

pinch of freshly grated nutmeg

salt and pepper

Dippers

fresh crusty bread, cut into
    bite-size pieces

small pieces of blanched asparagus

1 Rub the inside of a flameproof fondue pot with the garlic. Discard the garlic. Pour in the wine, then add 3 tablespoons of the brandy, transfer to the stove, and bring to a gentle simmer over low heat.

2 Add a handful of grated cheese and stir constantly until melted. Continue to add the cheese gradually, stirring constantly after each addition. Repeat until all the cheese has been added and stir until thoroughly melted and bubbling gently.

3 In a bowl, mix the cornstarch with the remaining brandy. Stir into the fondue and continue to stir for 3–4 minutes, or until thickened and bubbling. Stir in the nutmeg and season to taste.

4 Using protective mitts, transfer the fondue pot to a lit tabletop burner. To serve, invite your guests to spear pieces of bread and asparagus onto fondue forks and dip them into the fondue.

Cook's tip
These three cheeses are very similar. In all cases, avoid any that have too many holes or are bulging. However, signs of moisture around the holes indicate that they are in good condition.

Variation
You can substitute kirsch, a brandy distilled from cherries, for the brandy, but don't use cherry brandy.

FRENCH CHEESE WITH POTATO & BROCCOLI

The fresh aroma and almost fruity flavor of Beaufort cheese combines superbly with the rich creaminess of Camembert.

Serves 4

Preparation time: 25 minutes, plus 20 minutes' cooling

Cooking time: 1 hour 25 minutes

Ingredients

2 scallions, trimmed and
  chopped
2¼ cups dry white wine
12 oz/350 g Beaufort or
  Gruyère cheese, grated
12 oz/350 g Camembert
  cheese, rind removed, cut
  into small pieces

2 tbsp cornstarch
pinch of cayenne pepper
salt and pepper

Crispy potato skins
1 lb 10 oz/750 g medium
  potatoes
3 tbsp butter, melted
salt and pepper

Dippers
warm garlic bread or crusty
  French bread, cut into bite-
  size pieces
blanched broccoli flowerets

1 For the potato skins, preheat the oven to 400°F/200°C. Scrub the potatoes, pierce with a fork, and bake for 50 minutes. Let cool. Cut each lengthwise into 8 pieces. Scoop out most of the flesh, brush with butter, and season with salt and pepper. Arrange skin-side down on a cookie sheet. Bake for 12–15 minutes, or until crisp.

2 Put the scallions into a flameproof fondue pot with all but 2 tablespoons of the wine. Transfer to the stove and bring to a simmer over low heat. Add a handful of cheese and stir until melted. Repeat until all the cheese has been added.

3 In a bowl, mix the cornstarch with the remaining wine, stir into the fondue, and continue to stir for 3–4 minutes, or until thickened and bubbling. Stir in the cayenne and salt and pepper to taste. Using protective mitts, transfer the fondue pot to a lit tabletop burner. To serve, invite your guests to spear potato skins, bread, and broccoli onto fondue forks and dip them into the fondue.

Cook's tip
Ripe Camembert goes off very quickly, so do not buy it too far in advance. Choose one that is plump and soft but not runny.

Variation
If Beaufort cheese is not available, substitute the same quantity of Swiss cheese, as it's quite similar in flavor and texture.

MUSHROOM WITH POTATO & GARLIC BREAD

This unusual and delicious combination makes this fondue very satisfying and the perfect choice for cheering up a miserable winter evening.

Serves 4

Preparation time: 15 minutes

Cooking time: 25 minutes

Ingredients

3 tbsp butter

3 1/2 oz/100 g white mushrooms, diced

3 1/2 oz/100 g cremini or portabello
   mushrooms, diced

salt and pepper

1 tbsp chopped fresh parsley

1 garlic clove, finely chopped

2 cups dry white wine

12 oz/350 g Brie, rind removed,
   cut into small pieces

12 oz/350 g Beaufort or Gruyère
   cheese, grated

2 tbsp cornstarch

2 tbsp brandy

Dippers

warm garlic bread, cut into bite-size pieces

baby new potatoes, steamed

small whole mushrooms, lightly sautéed

1 Melt the butter in a skillet over medium heat. Add the diced mushrooms and cook, stirring, for 3–4 minutes, or until tender. Season to taste with salt and pepper, then stir in the parsley. Remove from the heat and set aside.

2 Put the garlic into a flameproof fondue pot and pour in the wine. Transfer to the stove and bring to a gentle simmer over low heat. Add a handful of cheese and stir constantly until melted. Continue to add the cheese gradually, stirring constantly after each addition. Repeat until all the cheese has been added. Stir in the mushroom mixture in small batches, until thoroughly incorporated.

3 In a bowl, mix the cornstarch with the brandy. Stir into the fondue. Continue to stir for 3–4 minutes, or until thickened and bubbling. Taste and adjust the seasoning if necessary. Using protective mitts, transfer the fondue pot to a lit tabletop burner. To serve, invite your guests to spear garlic bread, potatoes, and mushrooms onto fondue forks and dip them into the fondue.

Cook's tip
Steam the baby potatoes in their skins and peel them afterward as soon as they're cool enough to handle.

Variation
You could substitute shiitake mushrooms for all or some of the white mushrooms, as they have a strong, distinctive flavor and cook quickly.

SMOKED CHEDDAR WITH HAM & APPLES

These ingredients are just meant to go together, as the fruity flavor of hard cider cuts through the sharp tang of the cheese.

 Serves 4

Preparation time: 10 minutes

Cooking time: 15 minutes

Ingredients

2 tbsp lime juice

2 cups dry hard cider

1 lb 9 oz/700 g smoked Cheddar
   cheese, grated

2 tbsp cornstarch

pinch of ground allspice

salt and pepper

Dippers

4 apples, cored and cut into bite-size cubes,
   then brushed with lemon juice

fresh crusty bread, cut into bite-size cubes

canned pineapple chunks, drained

lean cooked ham, cut into bite-size cubes

1 Put the lime juice and all but 2 tablespoons of the hard cider into a large pan and bring to a gentle simmer over low heat. Add a handful of the cheese and stir until melted. Add the remaining cheese gradually, stirring constantly after each addition.

2 In a bowl, mix the cornstarch with the remaining hard cider, then stir into the pan. Continue to stir for 3–4 minutes, or until thickened and bubbling. Stir in the allspice and add salt and pepper to taste.

3 Pour the mixture into a fondue pot and, using protective mitts, transfer to a lit tabletop burner. To serve, invite your guests to spear pieces of apple, bread, pineapple, and ham onto fondue forks and dip them into the fondue.

Cook's tip
To emphasize the fruity flavor of this fondue, buy Cheddar cheese that has been smoked over apple wood.

Variation
Substitute the Swiss cheese Appenzeller for half the Cheddar, especially if you can find one where the rind has been washed in hard cider rather than wine.

SPANISH MANCHEGO WITH CHORIZO & OLIVES

*The buttery, nutty flavor of this cheese contrasts deliciously
with the spicy sausage and piquant olive dippers.*

○ Serves 4
Preparation time: 10–15 minutes
Cooking time: 15–20 minutes

Ingredients

1 garlic clove, peeled and halved

2 cups Spanish dry white wine

grated rind of 1 lemon or lime

1 lb 9 oz/700 g manchego cheese, grated

2 tbsp cornstarch

salt and pepper

Dippers

fresh crusty bread, cut into bite-size pieces

chorizo sausage, cut into bite-size pieces
    and lightly fried in olive oil

whole green and black olives, pitted

1 Rub the inside of a flameproof fondue pot with the garlic.
Discard the garlic. Pour in the white wine and add the lemon rind,
then transfer to the stove and bring to a gentle simmer over low
heat.

2 Toss the cheese in the cornstarch, then gradually stir the cheese
into the heated liquid, stirring constantly, until the cheese has
melted and the liquid is gently bubbling. Stir until thick and creamy.
Season to taste with salt and pepper.

3 Using protective mitts, transfer the fondue pot to a lit tabletop
burner. To serve, invite your guests to spear bread, chorizo, and
olives onto fondue forks and dip them into the fondue.

Cook's tip
*For an authentic flavor, look for Spanish olives. The best-
known green variety is Manzanilla, and Gordal olives—
either black or green—are also widely available.*

Variation
*If you find chorizo too spicy, substitute jamón serrano, a
sweet Spanish cured ham, a little like the Italian prosciutto.*

BASIL & FONTINA

This fragrant, creamy fondue is so evocative of the Mediterranean that its aroma alone will transport you to its sun-kissed shores.

 Serves 4

Preparation time: 15 minutes

Cooking time: 15–20 minutes

Ingredients

1¼ oz/35 g fresh basil, finely chopped

3 garlic cloves, finely chopped

10½ oz/300 g fontina cheese, chopped

9 oz/250 g ricotta cheese

1¾ oz/50 g Parmesan cheese, grated

2 tbsp lemon juice

generous 1½ cups vegetable stock

1 tbsp cornstarch

salt and pepper

Dippers

fresh Italian bread, such as ciabatta or focaccia,
    cut into bite-size pieces

selection of lightly cooked vegetables,
    cut into bite-size pieces

1 Put the basil and garlic into a large mixing bowl. Add all the cheeses and stir together well.

2 Put the lemon juice and all but 2 tablespoons of the stock into a large pan and bring to a gentle simmer over low heat. Add a small spoonful of the cheese mixture and stir constantly until melted. Continue to add the cheese mixture gradually, stirring constantly after each addition. Repeat until all the cheese mixture has been added and stir until thoroughly melted and bubbling gently. Mix the cornstarch with the remaining stock, then stir into the pan. Continue to stir for 3–4 minutes, or until thickened and bubbling. Season to taste with salt and pepper.

3 Pour the mixture into a fondue pot and, using protective mitts, transfer to a lit tabletop burner. To serve, invite your guests to spear pieces of bread and vegetables onto fondue forks and dip them into the fondue.

Cook's tip
If you're planning to use bouillon cubes or powder, try to find a brand that is not high in salt. As cheese is also salty, a salty stock would probably spoil the delicate flavor.

Variation
You can substitute other herbs for the basil for a different flavor. Try flat-leaf parsley, mint, or arugula.

RED BELL PEPPER & GARLIC

Broiling the bell peppers gives them a sweetness that goes beautifully with the surprisingly delicate flavor of this goat cheese.

Serves 4

Preparation time: 15 minutes

Cooking time: 35 minutes

Ingredients

2 red bell peppers, cut into quarters
   and seeded
1 large garlic clove, finely chopped
generous 1 cup dry white wine
14 oz/400 g Gruyère cheese, grated
2¾ oz/75 g Montrachet cheese,
   or other goat cheese if unavailable,
   cut into small pieces

1 tbsp cornstarch
1 tbsp chopped fresh parsley
salt and pepper

Dippers

whole green and black olives, pitted
fresh crusty bread, cut into bite-size pieces
roasted zucchini, cut into bite-size pieces
red bell peppers, cut into bite-size pieces

1 To skin the bell peppers, flatten them and arrange skin-side up on a broiler rack lined with foil. Broil for 10–15 minutes, or until the skins are blackened. Transfer to a plastic bag, set aside for 15 minutes, then peel off the skins. Cut 6 pieces into chunks and reserve for dippers. Dice the remainder.

2 Put the garlic and all but 2 tablespoons of the wine into a pan and bring to a gentle simmer over low heat. Add a handful of the Gruyère cheese and stir until melted. Add the remaining Gruyère gradually, stirring constantly after each addition. Add the diced bell peppers, then stir in the Montrachet until melted.

3 In a bowl, mix the cornstarch with the remaining wine, add to the pan, and stir for 3–4 minutes, or until thickened and bubbling. Stir in the parsley and salt and pepper to taste. Pour into a fondue pot, and, using protective mitts, transfer to a lit tabletop burner. To serve, invite your guests to spear olives, bread, bell pepper chunks, and zucchini onto fondue forks and dip them into the fondue.

Cook's tip
Montrachet is easy to recognize. It is ripened for a few days wrapped in chestnut or grape leaves and remains in this wrapping for sale.

Variation
You can substitute orange or yellow bell peppers for the red ones, but green bell peppers are probably too sharp for this dish.

EXOTIC MUSHROOMS & HERBS WITH VEGETABLES

Packed with flavor and fragrance yet subtle and delicate,

this is simply sensational and will prove irresistible.

🍽 Serves 4

🥣 Preparation time: 15–20 minutes

🍳 Cooking time: 25 minutes

Ingredients

2 tbsp butter

7 oz/200 g mixed exotic mushrooms, such as
   shiitake, chanterelle, and morel, coarsely sliced

salt and pepper

1 tbsp chopped fresh parsley

1 tbsp chopped fresh oregano

2 scallions, trimmed and finely chopped

¾ cup vegetable stock

3 tbsp lemon juice

¾ cup dry white wine

10½ oz/300 g fontina cheese, chopped

10½ oz/300 g Emmental cheese, grated

1 tbsp cornstarch

Dippers

fresh crusty bread, cut into bite-size pieces

selection of lightly cooked vegetables, cut
   into bite-size pieces

1 Melt the butter in a skillet over medium heat. Add the mushrooms and cook, stirring, for 3–4 minutes, or until tender. Season to taste with salt and pepper, then stir in the herbs. Remove from the heat.

2 Put the scallions into a flameproof fondue pot and pour in the stock, lemon juice, and all but 2 tablespoons of the wine. Transfer to the stove and bring to a gentle simmer over low heat. Add a handful of cheese and stir until thoroughly melted and bubbling gently. Repeat until all the cheese has been added and stir until melted. Stir in the mushroom mixture in small batches, until thoroughly incorporated.

3 In a bowl, mix the cornstarch with the remaining wine, then stir into the fondue. Continue to stir for 3–4 minutes, or until thickened and bubbling. Taste and adjust the seasoning if necessary. Using protective mitts, transfer the fondue pot to a lit tabletop burner. To serve, invite your guests to spear bread and vegetables onto fondue forks and dip them into the fondue.

Cook's tip
Try to avoid washing mushrooms as they are liable to absorb a lot of water, rather like a sponge. Simply wipe them clean with a damp cloth.

Variation
If fresh oregano is not available, use 1 teaspoon dried, as this is a herb that dries very successfully. However, do not use dried parsley, which is unappetizing.

GREEK CHEESE WITH OLIVES, PITA & BELL PEPPERS

The Greeks may not have invented fondue but this combination of sharp-tasting feta and aniseed-flavored ouzo is a great late entry.

 Serves 4

Preparation time: 15 minutes

Cooking time: 20 minutes

Ingredients

1 large garlic clove, finely chopped

1 cup Greek dry white wine

14 oz/400 g Emmental cheese, grated

2¾ oz/75 g feta cheese (drained weight), crumbled

1½ tbsp cornstarch

2 tbsp ouzo

1 tbsp chopped fresh cilantro

salt and pepper

Dippers

whole dark kalamata olives, pitted

warmed garlic pita bread, cut into bite-size pieces

skinned red bell peppers (see page 25), cut into bite-size pieces

1 Put the garlic and all but 2 tablespoons of the wine into a large pan and bring to a gentle simmer over low heat. Add a handful of the Emmental cheese and stir until melted. Add the remaining Emmental gradually, stirring constantly after each addition. Add the feta cheese and stir until melted.

2 In a bowl, mix the cornstarch with the ouzo, then stir into the pan. Continue to stir for 3–4 minutes, or until thickened and bubbling. Stir in the cilantro and add salt and pepper to taste.

3 Pour the mixture into a fondue pot and, using protective mitts, transfer to a lit tabletop burner. To serve, invite your guests to spear olives, pita bread, and red bell pepper onto fondue forks and dip them into the fondue.

Cook's tip
For the best flavor, try to find feta made with sheep's milk. Much of it nowadays is made with pasteurized cow's milk, but the original version is still produced in Greece and some other European countries.

Variation
If ouzo is not available, substitute a pastis, such as Ricard, as the aniseed flavor is essential. At a pinch, you can use Pernod, which is flavored with star anise.

THREE-CHEESE & BRANDY WITH SWEET ONIONS

Take one rich, nutty cheese, one mild, milky cheese, and one full-flavored creamy cheese and combine with sweet, golden pearl onions—sheer magic.

🍽 Serves 4

🥄 Preparation time: 15–20 minutes

🧤 Cooking time: 40 minutes

Ingredients

1 garlic clove, finely chopped

generous 1¾ cups dry white wine

9 oz/250 g sharp Cheddar cheese, grated

9 oz/250 g Monterey Jack cheese, grated

7 oz/200 g Brie, rind removed and cut into small pieces

1 tbsp cornstarch

2 tbsp brandy

salt and pepper

Sweet onions

1 tbsp butter

1 tbsp olive oil

9 oz/250 g baby onions, peeled but left whole

1 tsp superfine sugar

1 tsp balsamic vinegar

Dippers

warm garlic bread, cut into bite-size pieces

1 For the sweet onions, melt the butter and oil in a skillet over medium heat. Add the onions and cook, stirring, for 10 minutes. Sprinkle over the sugar and cook for 5 minutes. Stir in the vinegar and cook for an additional 5 minutes. Remove from the heat.

2 Put the garlic into a flameproof fondue pot and pour in the wine. Transfer to the stove and bring to a gentle simmer over low heat. Add a handful of cheese and stir until melted. Continue to add the cheese gradually, stirring constantly after each addition. Repeat until all the cheese has been added. Stir until thoroughly melted and bubbling gently.

3 In a bowl, mix the cornstarch with the brandy. Stir into the fondue and continue to stir for 3–4 minutes, or until thickened and bubbling. Season to taste with salt and pepper. Using protective mitts, transfer the fondue pot to a lit tabletop burner. To serve, invite your guests to spear the sweet onions, garlic bread, and vegetables onto fondue forks and dip them into the fondue.

Cook's tip
Balsamic vinegar has a unique, mellow flavor and can be produced only in a specified area around the Italian city of Modena. It is expensive but you need only a small amount in any dish, including this one.

Variation
Although it is not so easy to find, try using Teleme cheese from California instead of the Monterey Jack.

BLUE CHEESE WITH HAM-WRAPPED DIPPERS

Blue cheese rarely features in fondue recipes, but it's worth discovering for yourself the well-kept secret of its piquant perfection.

 Serves 4

Preparation time: 10–15 minutes

Cooking time: 15–20 minutes

Ingredients

1 garlic clove, peeled and halved

generous 1¾ cups dry white wine

5 tbsp brandy

12 oz/350 g Gruyère cheese, grated

12 oz/350 g Gorgonzola cheese, crumbled

1 tbsp cornstarch

2 tbsp light cream

salt and pepper

Dippers

fresh crusty bread, cut into bite-size pieces

bite-size pieces of lightly cooked vegetables
    wrapped in cooked ham or strips of lightly
    cooked bacon

1 Rub the inside of a flameproof fondue pot with the garlic. Discard the garlic. Pour in the wine and 3 tablespoons of the brandy, then transfer to the stove and bring to a gentle simmer over low heat. Add a handful of cheese and stir constantly until melted. Continue to add the cheese gradually, stirring constantly after each addition, until all the cheese has been added. Stir until thoroughly melted and bubbling gently.

2 In a bowl, mix the cornstarch with the remaining brandy. Stir into the fondue and continue to stir the mixture for 3–4 minutes, or until thickened and bubbling. Stir in the cream and season to taste.

3 Using protective mitts, transfer the fondue pot to a lit tabletop burner. To serve, invite your guests to spear bread and ham-wrapped vegetables onto fondue forks and dip them into the fondue.

Cook's tip
Blue cheese should never have a bitter or unpleasant smell and should have a creamy texture. Avoid buying any that is hard or discolored.

Variation
Other blue cheeses that would work well include Roquefort, Danablu, and Bleu de Bresse.

ITALIAN CHEESE WITH MEAT

Italians are proud of their cheese-making tradition and this fabulous fondue more than adequately demonstrates that they have every right to be.

Serves 4

Preparation time: 10–15 minutes

Cooking time: 15 minutes

Ingredients

1 garlic clove, peeled and halved

2 cups milk

3 tbsp brandy

10½ oz/300 g Gorgonzola cheese, crumbled

7 oz/200 g fontina cheese, chopped

7 oz/200 g mozzarella cheese, chopped

1 tbsp cornstarch

salt and pepper

Dippers

fresh Italian bread, cut into
    bite-size pieces

salami, cut into bite-size pieces

small pieces of apple, wrapped
    in prosciutto

morsels of roast chicken

1 Rub the inside of a flameproof fondue pot with the garlic. Discard the garlic. Pour in the milk and 1 tablespoon of the brandy, then transfer to the stove and bring to a gentle simmer over low heat. Add a handful of cheese and stir constantly until melted. Continue to add the cheese gradually, stirring constantly after each addition. Repeat until all the cheese has been added and stir until thoroughly melted and bubbling gently.

2 In a bowl, mix the cornstarch with the remaining brandy. Stir into the fondue and continue to stir the mixture for 3–4 minutes, or until thickened and bubbling. Season to taste with salt and pepper.

3 Using protective mitts, transfer the fondue pot to a lit tabletop burner. To serve, invite your guests to spear pieces of bread, salami, prosciutto-wrapped apple, and chicken onto fondue forks and dip them into the fondue.

Cook's tip
Mozzarella made from buffalo milk has a finer flavor than that made from cow's milk and is the best choice for eating fresh and uncooked. However, for cooking, day-old mozzarella is better and the cow's milk variety is fine.

Variation
Grissini—Italian breadsticks—also make good dippers for this fondue. Nowadays, they are available in a variety of flavors.

PINK CHAMPAGNE & CREAM

*Eating fondue always feels like a party and this recipe is especially festive,
particularly if you serve glasses of pink champagne with it.*

Serves 4
Preparation time: 10 minutes
Cooking time: 15 minutes

Ingredients

1¾ cups pink champagne

10½ oz/300 g Gruyère cheese, grated

10½ oz/300 g Crottin de Chavignol
   cheese, or other goat cheese if
   unavailable, cut into small pieces

1 tbsp cornstarch

2 tbsp light cream

salt and pepper

Dippers

fresh crusty bread, cut into
   bite-size pieces

whole white seedless grapes

1 Pour the champagne into a flameproof fondue pot. Transfer to the stove and bring to a gentle simmer
over low heat. Add a handful of Gruyère cheese and stir constantly until melted. Continue to add the
Gruyère gradually, stirring constantly after each addition. Repeat until all the Gruyère has been added and
stir until thoroughly melted and bubbling gently. Stir in the Crottin de Chavignol cheese until melted.

2 In a bowl, mix the cornstarch with the cream. Stir into the fondue and continue to stir for 3–4 minutes, or
until thickened and bubbling. Season to taste with salt and pepper.

3 Using protective mitts, transfer the fondue pot to a lit tabletop burner. To serve, invite your guests to spear
pieces of bread and grapes onto fondue forks and dip them into the fondue.

Cook's tip
*The trick to opening a champagne bottle is to take the
bottle from the cork, not the cork from the bottle. This
technique avoids both flying corks and spilt wine.*

Variation
*If champagne seems too extravagant, substitute a sparkling
wine. If using white wine, choose one that isn't extra dry.*

CHAPTER 2: STOCK FONDUES

RAVIOLI WITH RED WINE STOCK

*Providing your guests with a whole meal on a fork must be
one of the easiest and most delightful ways to entertain.*

Serves 4

Preparation time: 50 minutes

Cooking time: 1 ¼ hours

Stock

1 garlic clove, chopped

2 onions, chopped

2 celery stalks

3 large carrots, peeled and
chopped

1 quart water

1 bay leaf

3 fresh parsley sprigs

salt and pepper

3 tbsp red wine

Ravioli

1 lb/450 g durum wheat flour

4 eggs, beaten

2 tbsp olive oil

1 onion, finely chopped

4 tomatoes, peeled and finely
chopped

3 ½ oz/100 g mushrooms,
finely chopped

7 oz/200 g spinach leaves,
blanched and finely chopped

1 ¾ oz/50 g Parmesan cheese,
grated

2 tbsp chopped fresh basil

Dippers

selection of blanched
vegetables,
cut into bite-size pieces

1 For the ravioli, sift the flour in a mound onto a clean counter. Make a well in the center. Add the eggs
and half the oil. Mix together well. Knead for 10 minutes. Set aside for 30 minutes. Halve, then roll out
thinly into 2 rectangles. Cover with a damp dish towel.

2 In a skillet, cook the onion, tomatoes, and mushrooms in the remaining oil over medium heat for 8–10
minutes, or until the liquid has evaporated. Mix with the remaining ingredients. Place spoonfuls at intervals
on one pasta rectangle. Cover with the other rectangle, cut into squares around the mounds, and seal.
Cover with a damp dish towel.

3 Bring the stock ingredients to a boil in a pan. Reduce the heat and simmer for 1 hour. Strain into a
heatproof bowl. Discard the solids. Pour into a flameproof fondue pot until two-thirds full, then bring to
boiling point. Using protective mitts, transfer to a lit tabletop burner. To serve, invite your guests to spear
the ravioli and vegetables onto fondue forks and dip into the stock until cooked.

Cook's tip
*To peel tomatoes, place them in a heatproof bowl, add
boiling water to cover, and let stand for 2–3 minutes until
the skins split. Drain and refresh under cold water, then pull
off the skins with your fingers.*

Variation
*To color the pasta green, cook 3 ⅓ cups frozen spinach
according to the packet instructions, drain, and squeeze
out as much liquid as possible. Process in a blender or
food processor with the eggs, then add to the flour.*

CREAMY SAFFRON SCALLOPS

Bite-size shellfish make perfect dippers for this creamy fondue flavored—
and prettily colored—with aromatic saffron.

🍽 Serves 4

🥣 Preparation time: 15 minutes

♡ Cooking time: 25 minutes

Ingredients

2 lb 4 oz/1 kg live mussels

2 tbsp butter

2 garlic cloves, chopped

4 scallions, trimmed and chopped

1 quart dry white wine

½ cup water

1 bay leaf

generous 1 cup light cream

½ tsp ground saffron or turmeric

salt and pepper

Dippers

7 oz/200 g raw shelled scallops

selection of blanched vegetables,
   cut into bite-size pieces

1 Soak the mussels in lightly salted water for 10 minutes, then scrub the shells under cold running water. Pull off any beards. Discard any mussels with broken shells or that refuse to close when tapped.

2 Melt the butter in a large pan over low heat. Add the garlic and scallions and cook for 3 minutes, stirring constantly. Add the wine, water, bay leaf, and mussels, bring to a boil, and cook over high heat for 4 minutes, until the mussels have opened. Discard any that remain closed. Strain the mussels, reserving the liquid, and shell. Discard the bay leaf. Arrange the mussels with the dippers on serving plates.

3 Pour the liquid into a flameproof fondue pot until two-thirds full. Transfer to the stove and bring to boiling point over medium heat. Stir in the cream, saffron, and salt and pepper to taste. Using protective mitts, transfer the fondue pot to a lit tabletop burner. To serve, invite your guests to spear the dippers onto fondue forks and dip them into the hot fondue for 3–4 minutes, or until cooked.

Cook's tip
Before using the reserved mussel cooking liquid, it is
a good idea to strain it through a cheesecloth-lined
sieve to remove any traces of sand or grit.

Variation
Other seafood that would also be delicious with
this fondue includes thinly sliced raw abalone, clams,
cooked and shelled like the mussels, and cooked
peeled jumbo shrimp.

ASIAN FIREPOT WITH SEAFOOD DIPPERS

This recipe gives new meaning to the phrase "one-pot meal" as, when all the delicious seafood has been cooked, the stock is served with noodles as soup.

🍲 Serves 4

🥣 Preparation time: 20 minutes

🧤 Cooking time: 20 minutes

Ingredients

9 oz/250 g fine egg noodles

6½ cups fish or vegetable stock

2 garlic cloves, chopped

2 shallots, chopped

1 tbsp grated fresh gingerroot

1 tbsp grated fresh lemon grass

salt and pepper

1 tbsp rice wine or sherry

Dippers

10½ oz/300 g raw shrimp,
  shelled and deveined

7 oz/200 g raw shelled scallops

10½ oz/300 g sugar snap peas or
  snow peas, blanched

baby onions, peeled but left whole

1 quantity Asian Dipping Sauce
  (see page 66), to serve

1 Put the noodles into a heatproof bowl, cover with boiling water, and leave to soak for 4 minutes, then drain and set aside. Pour the stock into a large pan and add the garlic, shallots, gingerroot, lemon grass, and salt and pepper to taste. Bring to a boil, then reduce the heat and simmer for 15 minutes. Arrange the dippers on serving plates.

2 Stir the rice wine into the stock, then pour into a flameproof fondue pot (it should be no more than two thirds full). Using protective mitts, transfer the fondue pot to a lit tabletop burner. To serve, invite your guests to spear the dippers onto fondue forks, dip them into the hot stock until cooked to their taste, then dip them in the dipping sauce. When the dippers are finished, add the noodles to the stock and serve as a soup.

Cook's tip
To shell a scallop, hold it in one hand, flat side uppermost, insert a knife between the two shells, and cut the upper muscle. Separate the shells and slide the knife under the "skirt" to cut the lower muscle. Discard everything but the white part.

Variation
Monkfish fillet may be substituted for the shrimp. Cut it into bite-size chunks and parboil for 20–30 seconds, then drain, and refresh under cold water.

SHERRIED ROAST CHICKEN

The clever idea of using roast chicken for the dippers means only the vegetables have to cook in the stock, avoiding long delays between mouthfuls.

Serves 4

Preparation time: 15 minutes

Cooking time: 15 minutes

Ingredients

4 cups chicken stock

generous $\frac{1}{3}$ cup white wine

1 large garlic clove, chopped

1 tsp sugar

4 tbsp sherry

Dippers

1 lb 10 oz/750 g roast chicken breast, cut into
   bite-size pieces

2 red bell peppers, skinned (see page 25) and
   cut into bite-size pieces

blanched broccoli and cauliflower flowerets

peeled, blanched carrots, cut into bite-size pieces

1 quantity Aïoli (see page 67), to serve

1 Pour the stock into a large pan and add the wine, garlic, and sugar. Bring to a boil, then reduce the heat and simmer for 10 minutes. Arrange the dippers on serving plates.

2 Stir the sherry into the stock, then pour the stock into a flameproof fondue pot (it should be no more than two-thirds full). Using protective mitts, transfer the fondue pot to a lit tabletop burner. To serve, invite your guests to spear the dippers onto fondue forks, dip them into the hot stock until cooked to their taste, then dip them into the Aïoli.

Cook's tip

A medium sherry is probably the most suitable for this recipe. While it is best to use Spanish sherry rather than other "sherry-type wines," you don't have to use the best quality.

Variation

If you're not keen on garlic, make a quick-and-easy dip by stirring 2 tablespoons sun-dried tomato paste into 1 $\frac{1}{4}$ cups crème fraîche or strained plain yogurt.

SHABU SHABU

Like so many Japanese dishes, this is incredibly simple yet absolutely superb with a perfect balance of flavors and textures.

 Serves 4

Preparation time: 10–15 minutes

Cooking time: 5–10 minutes

Ingredients

4 cups beef stock

5-inch/13-cm piece kombu (dried kelp), cut into small pieces and rinsed in cold water

5 tbsp soy sauce

6 tbsp lime juice

14 oz/400 g precooked udon noodles, or rice noodles if unavailable

Dippers

1 lb 12 oz/800 g beef sirloin, cut into thin, bite-size strips

7 oz/200 g firm tofu or bean curd, cut into bite-size pieces

8 scallions, trimmed and cut into bite-size pieces

1 Pour the stock into a large pan and add the kombu. Bring to a boil, then reduce the heat and simmer for 5 minutes. Meanwhile, mix the soy sauce and lime juice in a small heatproof bowl, then stir in 1 tablespoon of stock from the pan and set aside. Arrange the dippers on serving plates.

2 Pour the stock and kombu into a flameproof fondue pot (it should be no more than two-thirds full). Using protective mitts, transfer the fondue pot to a lit tabletop burner. To serve, invite your guests to spear the dippers onto fondue forks or place them on heatproof spoons, dip them into the hot stock until cooked to their taste (cook the beef right through), then dip them in the soy sauce mixture. When all the dippers are finished, add the noodles to the stock in the fondue pot and serve as a soup.

Cook's tip
Japanese soy sauce, known as shoyu, is much less strongly flavored than Chinese. It is available from specialist food stores and some supermarkets.

Variation
You could substitute another popular Japanese seaweed, wakame, for the kombu. As it's also dried, soak it for 10 minutes in cold water first and then shred it.

KOMBU & SEAFOOD

The subtle flavor of this fondue and the colorful combination of the dippers form the perfect partnership for all lovers of seafood.

 Serves 4

Preparation time: 30 minutes

Cooking time: 5 minutes

Ingredients

5½ oz/150 g cellophane noodles

12 oz/350 g firm-fleshed fish fillets, such
   as cod, haddock, or angler fish, rinsed
   and cut into bite-size pieces

4 cups fish or vegetable stock

5-inch/13-cm piece kombu (dried kelp),
   cut into small pieces and rinsed in
   cold water

1 tbsp sake

6 tbsp soy sauce

Dippers

4 large peeled carrots, blanched and cut
   into bite-size pieces

1 lb/450 g raw shrimp, shelled and deveined

10½ oz/300 g sugar snap peas or
   snow peas, blanched

1 Put the noodles into a bowl, cover with cold water, and let soak for 30 minutes. Drain and cut into 3-inch/7.5-cm lengths. Meanwhile, bring a large pan of water to a boil, add the fish pieces, and cook briefly for 20 seconds. Drain, rinse under cold running water, and set aside.

2 Pour the stock into a large pan and add the kombu. Bring to a boil, then reduce the heat and simmer for 2 minutes. Pour in the sake. Arrange the fish on serving plates with the other dippers.

3 Pour the stock into a flameproof fondue pot (it should be no more than two-thirds full). Using protective mitts, transfer the fondue pot to a lit tabletop burner. To serve, invite your guests to spear the dippers onto fondue forks or place them on heatproof spoons, dip them into the hot stock until cooked to their taste, then dip them in the soy sauce. When all the dippers are finished, add the noodles to the stock and serve as a soup.

Cook's tip
Cellophane noodles are also known as glass, transparent, and bean thread noodles. They are made from mung beans. Dried noodles must always be soaked before cooking.

Variation
Sake, Japanese rice wine, varies considerably in price. If it seems rather expensive, then substitute mirin, sake produced specifically for cooking.

SPICY CHICKEN WITH BELL PEPPERS

A tantalizing treat to set the taste buds tingling, this is the ideal choice for lovers of hot and spicy food.

Serves 4

Preparation time: 1 1/2 hours

Cooking time: 20 minutes

Ingredients

4 tbsp chili oil

1 tbsp lemon juice

2 garlic cloves, chopped

1/2 tsp paprika

1/2 tsp turmeric

6 skinless, boneless chicken breasts, halved

salt and pepper

3 1/2 cups chicken stock

generous 1/3 cup red wine

1 fresh red chili, seeded and finely chopped

1 tbsp tomato paste

few drops of red food coloring (optional)

1 tbsp cornstarch

Dippers

whole cherry tomatoes

whole black olives, pitted

1 red bell pepper, skinned (see page 25) and

    cut into bite-size pieces

1 orange bell pepper, skinned (see page 25)

    and cut into bite-size pieces

freshly cooked rice, to serve

1 Put the oil, lemon juice, and half of the garlic into a large, shallow non-metallic dish. Rub the chicken with the paprika and turmeric, then add to the oil mixture with salt and pepper to taste. Turn until coated. Cover with plastic wrap and refrigerate for 1 1/2 hours.

2 Pour the stock into a large pan and pour in all but 2 tablespoons of the wine. Add the chili, tomato paste, remaining garlic, and the food coloring, if using. Bring to a boil, then reduce the heat and simmer for 10 minutes. Drain the chicken, cut into thin, bite-size slices, and arrange on serving plates with the dippers.

3 In a bowl, mix the cornstarch with the remaining wine. Stir into the pan. Continue to stir for 3–4 minutes, or until thickened. Pour into a flameproof fondue pot (no more than two-thirds full). Using protective mitts, transfer to a lit tabletop burner. To serve, invite your guests to spear the dippers onto fondue forks and dip into the stock until cooked (cook the chicken right through). Serve with rice.

Cook's tip
The heat in chilies is concentrated in the membranes surrounding the seeds rather than the seeds themselves. Seeding the chili gets rid of the membranes too.

Variation
Substitute about 900 g/2 lb thinly sliced pork tenderloin for the chicken. Cut it into bite-size pieces after marinating.

PORK WITH PEANUT SAUCE

Lime, chili, cilantro, lemongrass, plus a peanut sauce made with coconut milk—
this fondue is packed with the flavors of Southeast Asia.

 Serves 4

Preparation time: 1 ½ hours

Cooking time: 30 minutes

Ingredients

4 tbsp lime juice

3 tbsp chili oil

1 garlic clove, chopped

3 tbsp chopped fresh cilantro

1 lb 5 oz/600 g pork loin, cut
   into thin slices

4 scallions, trimmed and sliced

1 quart chicken or vegetable
   stock

1 tbsp grated fresh lemon grass

½ tsp chili powder

salt and pepper

Peanut sauce

generous 1 cup coconut milk

1 tsp red curry paste

4 tbsp smooth peanut butter

1 tsp grated fresh gingerroot

Dippers

7 oz/200 g firm tofu or bean
   curd, cut into bite-size pieces

selection of blanched vegetables,
   cut into bite-size pieces

freshly cooked noodles, to serve

1 Pour the lime juice into a large, shallow non-metallic dish. Add half of the oil, the garlic, cilantro, and pork. Turn the pork in the mixture, cover with plastic wrap, and refrigerate for 1 ¼ hours.

2 Heat the remaining oil in a large pan over medium heat. Add the scallions and cook, stirring, for 3 minutes. Add the stock, lemon grass, chili powder, and salt and pepper to taste. Bring to a boil, then reduce the heat and simmer for 25 minutes. Meanwhile, for the sauce, simmer the coconut milk in a separate pan for 15 minutes. Gradually stir in the remaining ingredients and simmer for 5 minutes. Drain the pork and thread onto wooden skewers.

3 Pour the stock mixture into a flameproof fondue pot (no more than two-thirds full). Using protective mitts, transfer to a lit tabletop burner. To serve, invite your guests to spear the dippers onto fondue forks and dip into the stock with the skewers until cooked (the pork should be cooked right through). Serve with noodles and the sauce.

Cook's tip
Coconut milk is widely available in cans. It is not the same thing as the liquid inside the nut, but is made from grated coconut flesh and water.

Variation
This fondue would also work well with thinly sliced sirloin steak, but don't substitute beef stock for the chicken or vegetable stock.

CHILI CHICKEN FIREPOT

*Thais love to share meals with family and friends and what
could be more sociable than this fragrant fondue?*

🍲 Serves 4

🥣 Preparation time: 1 ½ hours

🧤 Cooking time: 30 minutes

Ingredients

9 oz/250 g rice noodles

4 tbsp lemon juice

3 tbsp vegetable oil

1 fresh red chili, seeded and finely chopped

1 garlic clove, chopped

3 tbsp chopped fresh cilantro

6 skinless, boneless chicken breasts,
    cut into thin, bite-size slices

4 scallions, trimmed and sliced

1 quart chicken or vegetable stock

1 tbsp grated fresh lemon grass

½ tsp chili powder

salt and pepper

Dippers

selection of blanched vegetables, cut
    into bite-size pieces

whole cooked shelled shrimp

1 quantity Asian Dipping Sauce
    (see page 66), to serve

1 Put the noodles into a heatproof bowl, cover with boiling water, and soak for 4 minutes. Drain and set aside. Pour the lemon juice into a large, shallow non-metallic dish. Pour in half of the oil, then add the chili, garlic, cilantro, and chicken. Turn the chicken in the mixture (using heatproof spoons), cover with plastic wrap, and refrigerate for 1 ¼ hours.

2 Heat the remaining oil in a large pan over medium heat and cook the scallions, stirring, for 3 minutes. Add the remaining ingredients. Bring to a boil, then reduce the heat and simmer for 25 minutes. Drain the chicken. Arrange on serving plates with the dippers.

3 Pour the stock into a flameproof fondue pot (no more than two-thirds full). Using protective mitts, transfer to a lit tabletop burner. To serve, invite your guests to spear the dippers onto fondue forks, dip them into the hot stock until cooked (the chicken should be cooked right through), then dip in the dipping sauce. When the dippers are finished, add the noodles to the stock and serve as a soup.

Cook's tip
*For an authentic flavor, look for bird's eye or Thai chilies.
These are very tiny but do not be tempted to increase
the quantity as they are fiery hot.*

Variation
*If fresh lemongrass is not available, substitute the
same quantity of finely grated lemon rind.*

SCALLION & LEEK WITH TOFU

Very easy to make, tasty, and nutritionally balanced, this is the perfect choice for vegetarians who are getting tired of cheese.

🍽 Serves 4

🥣 Preparation time: 20 minutes

🧤 Cooking time: 1 hour 10 minutes

Ingredients

6 scallions, trimmed and chopped

1 leek, trimmed and sliced

2 celery stalks, chopped

3 large carrots, peeled and chopped

1 quart water

1 bouquet garni, made from fresh parsley, thyme,
   and rosemary sprigs, and a bay leaf

salt and pepper

1 garlic clove, peeled and halved

1 tbsp sherry

Dippers

7 oz/200 g firm tofu or bean curd, cut into
   bite-size pieces

selection of vegetables, such as broccoli flowerets
   and white mushrooms, and red bell peppers,
   cut into bite-size pieces

1 Put the scallions, leek, celery, carrots, and water into a large pan. Add the bouquet garni, season to taste with salt and pepper, and bring to a boil. Reduce the heat and simmer for 1 hour. Remove from the heat and strain through a strainer into a large heatproof bowl. Discard the solids and reserve the liquid. Arrange the dippers on a serving platter or individual plates ready for cooking.

2 Rub the inside of a flameproof fondue pot with the garlic. Discard the garlic. Pour in the reserved liquid until the fondue pot is two-thirds full, then transfer to the stove and bring to boiling point over medium heat. Stir in the sherry. Using protective mitts, transfer the fondue pot to a lit tabletop burner. To serve, invite your guests to spear the dippers onto fondue forks and dip them into the hot stock until cooked to their taste.

Cook's tip

Herbs are tied together into a bouquet garni to make them easier to remove. Sometimes a strip of celery is used to tie them. Alternatively, you can use kitchen string but the best way is to tie them inside a small square of cheesecloth.

Variation

For a non-vegetarian version, you could substitute cubes of cooked chicken or cooked, peeled jumbo shrimp for the tofu.

CHAPTER 3: SIZZLERS AND DIPPING SAUCES

MINI SPRING ROLLS

*The novelty of cooking their own spring rolls – and they
take very little time – is sure to delight your guests.*

	Serves 4
	Preparation time: 20 minutes
	Cooking time: 10 minutes

Ingredients

2 tbsp chili oil

4 scallions, trimmed and
   finely chopped

1 red bell pepper, seeded and
   finely sliced into 2-inch/5-cm
   lengths

1 carrot, peeled and finely
   sliced into 2-inch/5-cm
   lengths

3 oz/85 g bean sprouts

1 tbsp lemon juice

1 tsp soy sauce

salt and pepper

8 sheets phyllo pastry, halved

2 tbsp butter, melted

1 egg white, slightly beaten

4 cups peanut oil

Dippers

selection of vegetables, cut into
   bite-size pieces

To serve

1 quantity Asian Dipping Sauce
   (see page 66)

freshly cooked rice

1 Heat the chili oil in a wok or large skillet. Add the scallions, bell pepper, and carrot and stir-fry for 2
minutes. Add the bean sprouts, lemon juice, and soy sauce and stir-fry for 1 minute, then season to taste
and remove from the heat.

2 Spread out the pastry on a clean counter and brush with melted butter. Spoon a little of the vegetable
mixture onto one short end of each sheet of pastry, fold in the long sides, and roll up to enclose the filling.
Brush the edges with egg white to seal.

3 Pour the peanut oil into a metal fondue pot (no more than one-third full). Heat on the stove to
375°F/190°C, or until a cube of bread browns in 30 seconds. Using protective mitts, transfer the fondue
pot to a lit tabletop burner. To serve, invite your guests to spear the spring rolls and dippers onto fondue
forks and dip into the hot oil until cooked (the spring rolls will need 2–3 minutes). Drain off the excess oil.
Serve with the dipping sauce and rice.

Cook's tip
*As phyllo pastry dries out very quickly, it's best to keep the
sheets that you're not actually working on covered with a
damp dish towel.*

Variation
*You can fill the spring rolls with a wide variety of
ingredients including finely diced cooked chicken or pork
and small shrimp. Just be careful not to overfill them.*

CRISPY EDAM MELTS

This could be a messy business, but cooking these crisp, golden morsels will certainly turn out to be fun.

Serves 4

Preparation time: 15 minutes

Cooking time: 10 minutes

Ingredients

scant 2 cups all-purpose flour

$1/4$ tsp cayenne pepper

14 oz/400 g Edam cheese,
  rind removed and cut into
  bite-size cubes

1 tsp baking powder

1 tsp salt

2 large eggs

$1/2$ cup milk

4 cups peanut oil

Dippers

whole white mushrooms

whole cherry tomatoes

blanched broccoli flowerets

fresh mixed salad, to serve

1 Sift 150 g/5$1/2$ oz of the flour with the cayenne pepper into a large bowl. Add the cheese cubes and turn until coated. Shake off the excess flour, then arrange the cheese on a serving platter. Put the remaining flour into a large bowl with the baking powder and salt, then gradually beat in the eggs, milk and 1 tablespoon of the oil. Beat until the batter is smooth, then pour it into a serving bowl.

2 Pour the remaining oil into a metal fondue pot (it should be no more than one-third full), then heat on the hob to 190°C/375°F, or until a cube of bread browns in 30 seconds. Using protective gloves, carefully transfer the fondue pot to a lit tabletop burner.

3 To serve, allow your guests to spear the cheese cubes on to fondue forks, dip in the batter and let the excess run off, then cook in the hot oil for 1 minute, or until golden and crisp. Cook the other dippers in the same way, or leave them without batter and cook to your taste. Drain off the excess oil and serve with a mixed salad.

Cook's tip
If there is time, let the batter stand for 30 minutes before using to allow the starch grains to relax.

Variation
Try using other semihard cheeses, such as fontina, havarti, tilsit, or tomme de Savoie.

MIXED VEGETABLE TEMPURA

One of Japan's most famous dishes, this continues to be
popular with almost everyone—vegetarian or not.

Serves 4
Preparation time: 15 minutes
Cooking time: 15–20 minutes

Ingredients	Dippers
6 tbsp cornstarch	broccoli flowerets
6 tbsp soy sauce	white mushrooms
6 tbsp lemon juice	eggplant, cut into bite-size pieces
4 cups peanut oil	baby corn cobs, halved
1 egg	snow peas
1 cup ice water	cherry tomatoes
1 cup all-purpose flour	freshly cooked noodles, to serve

1 Put the cornstarch into a bowl and turn all the vegetable dippers in it until coated. Shake off the excess cornstarch, then arrange them on a serving platter. In a serving bowl, make a dipping sauce by mixing together the soy sauce and lemon juice, then set aside.

2 Pour the oil into a metal fondue pot (it should be no more than one-third full), then heat on the stove to 375°F/190°C, or until a cube of bread browns in 30 seconds. Using protective mitts, carefully transfer the fondue pot to a lit tabletop burner.

3 In a separate serving bowl, beat the egg and water together, then stir in the flour briefly. Do not overbeat: the batter should be lumpy. To serve, invite your guests to spear the dippers onto fondue forks, dip them in the batter, and let the excess run off, then cook in the hot oil for 2–3 minutes, or until cooked to their taste. Drain off the excess oil, then serve with the dipping sauce and noodles.

Cook's tip
There are two essentials that insure success with tempura. The water used to make the batter must be very cold and the oil should be heated to the specified temperature.

Variation
Other ingredients suitable for the tempura treatment are peeled raw jumbo shrimp, strips of squid, green beans, zucchini, and slices of bell pepper.

ASIAN DIPPING SAUCE

*A perfect balance of different flavors—sweet, sour, salty, and hot—
adds a delicious tang to seafood and meat fondues.*

🍽 Serves 4

🥣 Preparation time: 35–40 minutes

🧤 Cooking time: 7–8 minutes

Ingredients

generous ⅓ cup rice wine vinegar

finely grated rind and juice of 1 lime

2 tbsp soy sauce

1 ¼ cups sugar

1 tbsp grated fresh gingerroot

1 tbsp grated fresh lemon grass

2 garlic cloves, crushed

1 fresh red chili, seeded and
   finely chopped

2 tbsp sherry

1 tbsp chopped fresh cilantro

1 Put the vinegar, lime rind and juice, soy sauce, and sugar into a small pan and place over medium heat. Stir in the gingerroot, lemon grass, garlic, and chili and bring to a boil, stirring constantly. Reduce the heat and simmer, stirring, for 5 minutes.

2 Stir in the sherry and cilantro, heat through for an additional minute, then remove from the heat and strain through a strainer into a heatproof non-metallic serving bowl.

3 Let cool to room temperature, then serve.

Cook's tip
*Only the lower 5 inches of the lemon grass stalk is used
in cooking and it is important that it is finely grated
because it is very fibrous.*

Variation
*For an alternative dipping sauce, combine 2 crushed garlic
cloves and 2 seeded and sliced fresh red chilies in a
bowl, then stir in 3 tablespoons each lime juice and
dark soy sauce, and 1 tablespoon water.*

AÏOLI

This creamy garlic mayonnaise from Provence is the perfect partner for seafood, vegetables, and chicken.

Serves 4
Preparation time: 15 minutes
Cooking time: 0 minutes

Ingredients

3 large garlic cloves, finely chopped

2 egg yolks

1 cup extra virgin olive oil

1 tbsp lemon juice

1 tbsp lime juice

1 tbsp Dijon mustard

1 tbsp chopped fresh tarragon

salt and pepper

sprig of tarragon, to decorate

1 Ensure that the ingredients are all at room temperature. Put the garlic and the egg yolks into a food processor and process until well blended. With the motor running, pour in the oil teaspoon-by-teaspoon through the feeder tube until it starts to thicken, then pour in the remaining oil in a thin stream until a thick mayonnaise forms.

2 Add the lemon and lime juices, along with the mustard and tarragon, and season to taste with salt and pepper. Blend until smooth, then transfer to a non-metallic bowl. Decorate with a sprig of tarragon.

3 Cover with plastic wrap and refrigerate until needed.

Cook's tip
Don't be tempted to try to speed up the process by adding the oil more quickly as this will simply result in a curdled mess.

Variation
For a spicy mayonnaise, omit the garlic and add 1 teaspoon Worcestershire sauce and a dash of Tabasco sauce.

LIME & CHILI CRAB BALLS

A bite-size version of the perennially popular Thai favorite crab cakes, these are guaranteed to be a success.

 Serves 4

Preparation time: 1¼ hours

Cooking time: 15–20 minutes

Ingredients

1 lb/450 g frozen crabmeat, thawed

2 tbsp freshly grated lime rind

1 fresh red chili, seeded and finely chopped

1 tbsp finely chopped scallion

1 tbsp grated fresh gingerroot

1 tbsp grated fresh coconut

2 egg yolks

4 tsp cornstarch

4 tbsp thick plain yogurt

2 tbsp sherry

salt and pepper

4 cups peanut oil

Dippers

7 oz/200 g firm tofu or bean curd, cut into bite-size pieces

selection of vegetables, cut into bite-size pieces

To serve

1 quantity Asian Dipping Sauce (see page 66)

freshly cooked rice

1 Put the crabmeat, lime rind, chili, scallion, gingerroot, coconut, and egg yolk into a bowl and mix together well. Mix the cornstarch with the yogurt and sherry in a small pan, place over low heat, and stir until thickened. Remove from the heat, mix into the bowl with the crabmeat mixture, and season to taste with salt and pepper. Pull off pieces of the mixture and shape into 1-inch/2.5-cm balls. Cover with plastic wrap and chill for at least 1 hour. Arrange the other dippers on serving plates.

2 Pour the oil into a metal fondue pot (it should be no more than one-third full), then heat on the stove to 375°F/190°C, or until a cube of bread browns in 30 seconds. Using protective mitts, carefully transfer the fondue pot to a lit tabletop burner. To serve, invite your guests to spear the dippers onto fondue forks (place the crab balls on spoons if not firm enough to spear), then cook in the hot oil for about 2–3 minutes, or until cooked to their taste. Drain off the excess oil, then serve with the dipping sauce and rice.

Cook's tip
You can, of course, use fresh white crabmeat for this recipe if you like. Whether fresh or frozen, pick it over carefully first and remove any stray pieces of cartilage.

Variation
For a more economical version of this recipe, substitute finely chopped white fish fillet for the crabmeat.

ROMANO & CHILI TUNA SIZZLERS

This unusual fondue will surprise your guests when they come to cook it and delight them when they taste it.

Serves 4

Preparation time: 20 minutes

Cooking time: 15–20 minutes

Ingredients
2 tbsp grated romano cheese

2 eggs

5 tbsp all-purpose flour

6 oz/175 g canned tuna, flaked

1 tbsp grated fresh gingerroot

1 tbsp grated lemon rind

1 cup corn

$\frac{1}{2}$ tsp finely chopped fresh red chili

4 cups peanut oil

fresh mixed salad, to serve

Red chili dipping sauce
$\frac{1}{2}$ cup plain yogurt

4 tbsp mayonnaise

1 fresh red chili, seeded and finely chopped

1 tbsp lime juice

Dippers
selection of vegetables, cut into
   bite-size pieces

whole cooked shelled shrimp

1 Put the cheese, eggs, and flour into a large bowl and beat together. Add the tuna, gingerroot, lemon rind, corn, and the $\frac{1}{2}$ teaspoon of chopped red chili and stir together well. Meanwhile, for the sauce, put all the ingredients into a non-metallic serving bowl, mix together, and set aside. Arrange the dippers on serving plates.

2 Pour the oil into a metal fondue pot (it should be no more than one-third full), then heat on the stove to 375°F/190°C, or until a cube of bread browns in 30 seconds. Using protective mitts, carefully transfer the fondue pot to a lit tabletop burner. To serve, invite your guests to spear the dippers onto fondue forks and cook them with spoonfuls of the tuna mixture in the hot oil for 3 minutes, or until cooked to their taste. Drain off the excess oil, then serve with the dipping sauce and a mixed salad.

Cook's tip
Nowadays, tuna is available canned in olive oil, sunflower oil, brine, and spring water. Whichever you choose, make sure it is well drained.

Variation
You could also make this with canned salmon, which is much improved by the addition of the spicy flavorings.

CHICKEN & BACON SKEWERS

There's only one word for bacon-wrapped strips of chicken, a creamy mustard dip, and a selection of cooked and raw vegetables—scrumptious.

 Serves 4

Preparation time: 15 minutes

Cooking time: 15–20 minutes

Ingredients

½ tsp turmeric

6 skinless, boneless chicken
   breasts

salt and pepper

4 cups peanut oil

Mustard dip

4 tbsp sour cream

4 tbsp mayonnaise

2 tbsp whole-grain mustard

1 tsp honey

1 scallion, trimmed and finely
   chopped

pinch of paprika

Dippers

4 lean unsmoked bacon slices

cherry tomatoes

whole baby onions, peeled

white mushrooms

sautéed new potatoes and a
   fresh mixed salad, to serve

1 Rub the turmeric over the chicken breasts, then season and cut into strips. Stretch the bacon slices until doubled in length and cut into thin strips lengthwise. Roll up the slices of chicken and bacon and thread them onto wooden skewers with the other dippers, leaving plenty of space at either end. Skewer the tomatoes separately, because they will need less time time to cook. For the dip, mix all the ingredients in a bowl.

2 Pour the oil into a metal fondue pot (it should be no more than one-third full), then heat on the stove to 375°F/190°C, or until a cube of bread browns in 30 seconds. Using protective mitts, carefully transfer the fondue pot to a lit tabletop burner.

3 Invite your guests to dip the skewers into the fondue, and cook in the hot oil for 2–3 minutes, or until cooked (cook the chicken and bacon right through). Drain off the excess oil. Serve with sautéed potatoes, salad, and the dip.

Cook's tip
The easiest way to stretch strips of bacon is with the back of a knife. Don't be too heavy-handed or the meat will tear.

Variation
For extra flavor, spread each strip of chicken with a mixture of cream cheese and chives before rolling up.

MARINATED BEEF WITH ASIAN DIPPING SAUCE

Marinating the steak in a spicy mixture gives it a wonderful

flavor that's further enhanced by the dipping sauce.

 Serves 4

Preparation time: 1 1/2 hours

Cooking time: 15 minutes

Ingredients

6 tbsp soy sauce

5 tbsp dry sherry

1 garlic clove, chopped

1 tbsp grated fresh gingerroot

1 tsp sugar

1 lb 12 oz/800 g tenderloin steak,
   cut into thin, bite-size strips

4 cups peanut oil

Dippers

selection of vegetables, cut into
   bite-size pieces

To serve

1 quantity Asian Dipping Sauce
   (see page 66)

freshly cooked noodles

1 Put the soy sauce, sherry, garlic, gingerroot, and sugar into a large, shallow dish and mix together.
Add the strips of steak and turn them in the mixture. Cover with plastic wrap and refrigerate for 1 1/4 hours.

2 Drain the steak, pat dry with paper towels, and thread onto wooden skewers, leaving space at either
end. Arrange the skewers on serving plates with the other dippers.

3 Pour the oil into a metal fondue pot (it should be no more than one-third full), then heat on the stove to
375°F/190°C, or until a cube of bread browns in 30 seconds. Using protective mitts, carefully transfer
the fondue pot to a lit tabletop burner.

4 To serve, invite your guests to spear the dippers onto fondue forks and dip them into the hot oil with the
beef skewers until cooked to their taste (cook the beef right through). Drain off the excess oil, then serve
with the dipping sauce and noodles.

Cook's tip
*Dark soy sauce is sweeter than light and is the better
type to use for marinades. Light soy sauce is more
suitable as a condiment.*

Variation
*You could substitute the same quantity of pork tenderloin for
the steak, cutting it into thin strips in the same way.*

SIZZLING STEAK WITH RICH TOMATO SAUCE

*This is so succulent and richly flavored it's easy to see why
it is one of the world's best-loved meat fondues.*

Serves 4
Preparation time: 15–20 minutes
Cooking time: 45–50 minutes

Ingredients
1 lb 12 oz/800 g tenderloin
    steak, cut into ¾-inch/2-cm
    cubes
4 cups peanut oil
salt and pepper

Rich tomato sauce
1 tbsp olive oil
1 garlic clove, finely chopped
1 onion, finely chopped
14 oz/400 g canned
    chopped tomatoes
1 tbsp tomato paste
2 tbsp red wine
1 tbsp chopped fresh parsley
1 tbsp chopped fresh oregano

Dippers
baby onions, peeled but
    left whole
white mushrooms
cherry tomatoes
crusty French bread, to serve

1 For the tomato sauce, heat the olive oil in a small pan over medium heat, add the garlic and onion,
and cook, stirring, for 3 minutes, until softened. Stir in the tomatoes, tomato paste, and wine. Bring to a
boil, then reduce the heat and simmer gently, stirring occasionally, for about 25 minutes. Remove from the
heat, stir in the parsley and oregano, and set aside. Arrange the cubes of steak and the other dippers on
serving plates.

2 Pour the peanut oil into a metal fondue pot (it should be no more than one-third full), then heat on the
stove to 375°F/190°C, or until a cube of bread browns in 30 seconds. Using protective mitts, carefully
transfer the fondue pot to a lit tabletop burner.

3 To serve, invite your guests to spear the steak cubes and dippers onto fondue forks and dip them into the
hot oil until cooked (cook the steak right through). Drain off the excess oil. Season to taste with salt and
pepper. Serve with bread and the hot or cold sauce.

Cook's tip
*If you have time, it is worth marinating the steak in a
mixture of 1¼ cups red wine, 2 tablespoons red
wine vinegar, 2 tablespoons olive oil, 2 crushed garlic
cloves, and black pepper.*

Variation
*For a less expensive version of this fondue, substitute round
steak for the tenderloin steak and beat with a meat bat first.*

CHILI & CILANTRO PORK SATAY

The classic street food from Southeast Asia, cooked on skewers over charcoal, is given a new twist as a fondue.

Serves 4

Preparation time: 1 ½ hours

Cooking time: 20 minutes

Ingredients

2 tbsp lemon juice

3 tbsp vegetable oil

1 garlic clove, chopped

2 tbsp chopped fresh cilantro

1 tbsp grated fresh lemon grass

1 fresh red chili, seeded and
   finely chopped

1 lb 12 oz/800 g pork loin,
   cut into thin slices

4 cups peanut oil

salt and pepper

freshly cooked rice, to serve

Satay sauce

1 tsp chili oil

1 garlic clove, crushed

1 scallion, trimmed and
   finely chopped

1 fresh red chili, seeded and
   finely chopped

1 tsp Thai red curry paste

.5 tbsp crunchy peanut butter

generous 1 cup coconut milk

Dippers

selection of fresh vegetables, cut
   into bite-size pieces

1 Pour the lemon juice into a large, shallow non-metallic dish. Add the vegetable oil, garlic, cilantro, lemon grass, chili, and pork. Turn the pork in the mixture, cover with plastic wrap, and refrigerate for 1 ¼ hours. Drain the pork, pat dry with paper towels, and arrange on a serving platter with the other dippers.

2 For the sauce, heat the chili oil in a small pan, add the garlic and scallion, and cook, stirring, for 3 minutes. Stir in the remaining ingredients, bring to a boil, then reduce the heat to a simmer.

Cook's tip
In Indonesia and other Southeast Asian countries, tamarind would be used to provide the sourness in the marinade, but lemon juice is perfectly good and rather less effort.

Variation
Strips of skinless, boneless chicken breast and peeled, raw jumbo shrimp are also delicious cooked and served like this.

CRISPY-COATED PORK SAUSAGES

*Not just any old sausages, this delicious homemade version
with a crisp bread crumb coating is hard to beat.*

🍽 Serves 4

🥄 Preparation time: 25 minutes

🧤 Cooking time: 15–20 minutes

Ingredients

1 lb/450 g pork bulk sausage

1 small onion, grated

6 tbsp grated Cheddar cheese

1 tbsp tomato paste

1/2 cup fresh bread crumbs

1 tsp turmeric

1/2 tsp paprika

salt and pepper

2 eggs, beaten

generous 3/4 cup dried
    bread crumbs

4 cups peanut oil

Dippers

white mushrooms

eggplant, cut into bite-size
    pieces

To serve

1 quantity Mustard Dip (see
    page 72)

1 quantity Crispy Potato Skins
    (see page 16)

warm crusty bread

1 Put the bulk sausage into a large bowl with the onion, cheese, tomato paste, fresh bread crumbs, turmeric, and paprika and season to taste with salt and pepper. Mix together well and, using your hands, shape into small sausages about 2 inches/5 cm long. Turn them in the beaten egg, then coat them in dried bread crumbs. Arrange on a serving platter with the other dippers.

2 Pour the oil into a metal fondue pot (it should be no more than one-third full), then heat on the stove to 375°F/190°C, or until a cube of bread browns in 30 seconds. Using protective mitts, carefully transfer the fondue pot to a lit tabletop burner.

3 To serve, invite your guests to spear the pork sausages and other dippers onto fondue forks and dip into the hot oil until cooked to their taste (cook the sausages right through—they will need at least 3–4 minutes). Drain off the excess oil, then serve with the dip, bread, and Crispy Potato Skins.

Cook's tip
*The quickest and easiest way to make bread crumbs
is in a blender or food processor. Process in small
batches at a time.*

Variation
*For a summery flavor, substitute 1 tablespoon chopped
fresh thyme or 1 teaspoon dried thyme for the turmeric
and use sweet rather than hot paprika.*

CHAPTER 4: DESSERT FONDUES

BRANDY CHOCOLATE WITH FRUIT DIPPERS

There can be few more delicious ways to end a meal than the leisurely consumption of fruit dipped in a rich chocolate fondue.

🍽 Serves 4

🥣 Preparation time: 15–10 minutes

🧤 Cooking time: 10–15 minutes

Ingredients

9 oz/250 g bittersweet or unsweetened
   chocolate (must contain at least
   50 percent cocoa solids)

scant ½ cup heavy cream

2 tbsp brandy

Dippers

plain sponge cake, cut into bite-size pieces

small pink and white marshmallows

small firm whole fresh fruits, such as black currants,
   blueberries, cherries, and strawberries

whole no-soak dried apricots

candied citrus peel, cut decoratively into
   strips or bite-size pieces

1 Arrange the dippers decoratively on a serving platter or individual serving plates and set aside.

2 Break or chop the bittersweet chocolate into small pieces and place in the top of a double boiler or into a heatproof bowl set over a pan of simmering water. Pour in the heavy cream and stir until melted and smooth. Stir in the brandy, then carefully pour the mixture into a warmed fondue pot.

3 Using protective mitts, transfer the fondue pot to a lit tabletop burner. To serve, invite your guests to spear the dippers onto fondue forks and dip them into the fondue.

Cook's tip

When melting chocolate over simmering water it is important that the base of the bowl does not touch the surface of the water.

Variation

If you don't like brandy or want a change, try a liqueur with a flavor that complements chocolate, such as triple sec (orange) or crème de menthe (mint).

MOCHA WITH AMARETTI

As if the fabulous combination of chocolate and coffee were not enough, this luxurious fondue also includes heavy cream and liqueur.

 Serves 4

Preparation time: 5–10 minutes

Cooking time: 10–15 minutes

Ingredients

9 oz/250 g semisweet or unsweetened
  chocolate (must contain at least
  50 percent cocoa solids)

scant ½ cup heavy cream

1 tbsp instant coffee powder

3 tbsp coffee-flavored liqueur,
  such as Kahlúa

Dippers

cookies, such as amaretti

plain or coffee-flavored marbled cake or
  sponge cake, cut into bite-size pieces

whole seedless grapes

sliced firm peaches or nectarines

1 Arrange the dippers decoratively on a serving platter or individual serving plates and set aside.

2 Break or chop the chocolate into small pieces and place in the top of a double boiler or in a heatproof bowl set over a pan of simmering water. Add the cream and coffee powder and stir until melted and smooth. Stir in the liqueur, then carefully pour the mixture into a warmed fondue pot.

3 Using protective mitts, transfer the fondue pot to a lit tabletop burner. To serve, invite your guests to spear the dippers onto fondue forks and dip them into the fondue.

Cook's tip
You can melt semisweet chocolate on medium in the microwave. Break it into small pieces, place in a microwave safe bowl, leave it uncovered, and stir every 10 seconds.

Variation
Substitute 4 oz bittersweet chocolate for the same quantity of semisweet for a very sophisticated, adult flavor.

CREAMY RUM WITH BANANA

This richly flavored fondue with a hidden kick is seventh heaven for all lovers of sweet things.

Serves 4
Preparation time: 5–10 minutes
Cooking time: 10 minutes

Ingredients
2/3 cup superfine sugar
4 tbsp water
1 1/2 cups heavy cream, gently warmed
3 tbsp rum

Dippers
plain sponge cake, cut into
   bite-size pieces
firm ripe bananas, cut into
   bite-size pieces
sliced apples

1 Arrange the dippers decoratively on a serving platter or individual serving plates and set aside.

2 Put the sugar and water into a heavy-based pan, place over low heat, and stir until the sugar has dissolved. Bring to a boil, then let bubble for 3–4 minutes. Stir in the warmed cream and continue to stir for 4–5 minutes, or until smooth and well combined. Stir in the rum and cook for an additional minute. Remove from the heat and carefully pour the mixture into a warmed fondue pot.

3 Using protective mitts, transfer the fondue pot to a lit tabletop burner. To serve, invite your guests to spear the dippers onto fondue forks and dip them into the fondue.

Cook's tip
It is important that the cream is warmed before it is added to the pan as otherwise the caramel may not dissolve. However, don't bring it to a boil.

Variation
If you're serving this fondue to—supervised—children, substitute freshly squeezed orange juice for the rum.

VANILLA TOFFEE

Gloriously sticky and very self-indulgent, this an unusual and utterly delicious way to serve dessert.

🍽 Serves 4
🥣 Preparation time: 10 minutes
🥄 Cooking time: 10 minutes

Ingredients

4½ oz/125 g butter

2 cups brown sugar

1 cup corn syrup

2 tbsp maple syrup

2 tbsp water

1¾ cups canned condensed milk

1 tsp vanilla extract

½ tsp ground cinnamon

1 tbsp rum

Dippers

cookies

firm ripe bananas, cut into bite-size pieces

sliced apples

bite-size pieces of chocolate

miniature cakes

shelled nuts, such as pecans or Brazil nuts,
    and walnut halves

1 Arrange the dippers decoratively on a serving platter or individual serving plates and set aside.

2 Put the butter into a heatproof bowl set over a pan of simmering water and melt gently. Add the sugar, corn syrup, maple syrup, water, condensed milk, vanilla extract, and cinnamon. Stir until thickened and smooth, then stir in the rum and cook for an additional minute. Remove from the heat and carefully pour the mixture into a warmed fondue pot.

3 Using protective mitts, transfer the fondue pot to a lit tabletop burner. To serve, invite your guests to spear the dippers onto fondue forks and dip them into the fondue.

Cook's tip
Maple syrup is expensive but is worth it for its special flavor. Cheaper brands are often blended with corn or cane syrup and prove a false economy.

Variation
For a different flavor, substitute almond extract for the vanilla and provide macaroons for dipping.

NUTTY BUTTERSCOTCH WITH POPCORN

 A treat for children of all ages, this is a fail-safe way to persuade them to eat more fruit—but keep an eye on the younger ones.

Serves 4

Preparation time: 5–10 minutes

Cooking time: 10–15 minutes

Ingredients

1¾ cups brown sugar

½ cup water

1 tbsp rum

6 tbsp unsalted butter

½ cup heavy cream, gently warmed

generous ½ cup peanuts, chopped

Dippers

popcorn

firm ripe bananas, cut into
 bite-size pieces

sliced apples

1 Arrange the dippers decoratively on a serving platter or individual serving plates and set aside.

2 Put the sugar and water into a heavy-based pan, place over medium heat, and stir until the sugar has dissolved. Bring to a boil, then let bubble for 6–7 minutes. Stir in the rum and cook for an additional minute.

3 Using protective mitts, remove from the heat and carefully stir in the butter until melted. Gradually stir in the cream until the mixture is smooth. Finally, stir in the nuts.

4 Carefully pour the mixture into a warmed fondue pot, then transfer to a lit tabletop burner. To serve, invite your guests to spear the dippers onto fondue forks and dip them into the fondue.

Cook's tip
The easiest way to eat this is to spear the fruit onto forks and dip them in the fondue, then, when they are nice and sticky, roll the fruit in individual dishes of popcorn.

Variation
Other delicious dippers could include chunks of mango, kiwi fruit, and watermelon, and you could substitute crushed meringues for the popcorn.

CHOCOLATE WON TONS WITH MAPLE SAUCE

This imaginative dessert is surprisingly easy to prepare but there's no surprise about how easy it is to eat.

🍽 Serves 4

🥣 Preparation time: 5–10 minutes

♡ Cooking time: 10–15 minutes

Ingredients

16 won ton skins

12 oz/350 g semisweet
  chocolate, chopped

1 tbsp cornstarch

3 tbsp cold water

4 cups peanut oil

Maple sauce

¾ cup maple syrup

4 tbsp butter

½ tsp ground allspice

vanilla ice cream, to serve

1 Spread out the won ton skins on a clean counter, then spoon a little chocolate into the center of each. In a small bowl, mix together the cornstarch and water until smooth. Brush the edges of the skins with the mixture, then wrap into triangles, squares, or bundles and seal the edges. Arrange on a serving platter.

2 Put all the sauce ingredients into a pan and stir over medium heat. Bring to a boil, then reduce the heat and simmer for 3 minutes.

3 Meanwhile, pour the oil into a metal fondue pot (it should be no more than one-third full), then heat on the stove to 375°F/190°C, or until a cube of bread browns in 30 seconds. Using protective mitts, carefully transfer the fondue pot to a lit tabletop burner.

4 To serve, invite your guests to place the won tons onto metal spoons and dip them into the hot oil until cooked to their taste (they will need about 2–3 minutes). Drain off the excess oil, then serve the won tons with vanilla ice cream and the sauce.

Cook's tip
Won ton wrappers are paper-thin squares of yellow-colored dough and are widely available from Chinese supermarkets.

Variation
You can substitute other ice cream flavors for the vanilla, including tropical fruits, coffee, apricot, and orange.

Index

aïoli 67

asian fondues
   dipping sauce 66
   firepot with seafood dippers 44
   marinated beef with
      asian dipping sauce 74

basil and fontina 22
beaufort
   french cheese with potato & broccoli 16
   mushroom with potato & garlic bread 20
beef
   marinated beef with
      asian dipping sauce 66
   shabu shabu 47
   sizzling steak with rich tomato sauce 76
blue cheese with ham-wrapped dippers 32
brandy chocolate with fruit dippers 84
brie
   mushroom with potato & garlic bread 18
   three-cheese & brandy
      with sweet onions 30

camembert
   french cheese with potato & broccoli 16
cheddar
   smoked, with ham & apple 20
   three-cheese & brandy
      with sweet onions 30
chicken
   & bacon skewers 72
   chili firepot 54
   sherried roast 46
   spicy, with bell peppers 50
chili
   chicken firepot 54
   & cilantro pork satay 78
   lime & crab balls 68
   pork with peanut sauce 52
   romano & tuna sizzlers 70
chocolate
   brandy with fruit dippers 84
   won tons with maple sauce 94
crab, lime & chili balls 68
creamy fondues
   blue cheese with ham-wrapped dippers 32
   rum with banana 88
   saffron scallops 42
crispy dippers
   coated pork sausages 80

french cheese with potato & broccoli 60
   mini spring rolls 60
crottin de chavignol,
   pink champagne & cream 36

edam, crispy melts 62
emmental 8
   exotic mushroom & herbs
      with vegetables 26
   greek cheese with olives, pita
      & bell peppers 28
   gruyère with asparagus 14

fondue pots 9, 11
fontina 8
   basil & 22
   exotic mushroom & herbs
      with vegetables 26
   italian cheese with meat dippers 34
french cheese with potato & broccoli 16

gorgonzola
   blue cheese with ham-wrapped dippers 32
   italian cheese with meat dippers 34
greek cheese with olives,
   pita & bell peppers 28
gruyère 8
   with asparagus 14
   blue cheese with ham-wrapped dippers 32
   pink champagne & cream 36
   red bell pepper & garlic 24

hints 11

italian cheese with meat dippers 34

kombo & seafood 48

maple sauce 94
mixed vegetable tempura 64
mocha with amaretti 86
monterey jack, three-cheese & brandy
   with sweet onions 30
montrachet, red bell pepper & garlic 24
mozzarella, italian cheese
   with meat dippers 34
mushroom
   exotic, & herbs with vegetables 26
   with potato & garlic bread 18
mustard dip 72

nutty butterscotch with popcorn 92

parmesan
   basil & fontina 22
   gruyère with asparagus 14
peanut sauce 52
pink champagne & cream 36
pork
   chili & cilantro satay 78
   chili, with peanut sauce 52
   crispy-coated sausages 80
pots 9, 11

ravioli with red wine stock 40
red bell pepper & garlic 24
rich tomato sauce 76
ricotta, basil & fontina 22
romano & chili tuna sizzlers 70

satay sauce 79
sauces
   aïoli 67
   asian 66
   maple 94
   mustard 72
   peanut 52
   rich tomato 76
   satay 79
scallion & leek with tofu 56
   scallops, creamy saffron 42
shabu shabu 47
sherried roast chicken 46
sizzling steak with rich tomato sauce 76
smoked cheddar with ham & apple 20
spanish manchego with chorizo
   and olives 21
spicy chicken with bell peppers 50
spring rolls, mini 60
sweet onions 30
steak, sizzling, with rich tomato sauce 76

tempura, mixed vegetable 64
three-cheese & brandy with
   sweet onions 30
tips 11
tomato sauce, rich 76

vegetable tempura, mixed 64

vanilla toffee 90